D1205573

PEOPLE
WHO MADE
A DIFFERENCE

# LOUIS BRAILLE

Titles in the
**PEOPLE WHO MADE A DIFFERENCE**
series include

*Louis Braille*
*Marie Curie*
*Father Damien*
*Mahatma Gandhi*
*Bob Geldof*
*Martin Luther King, Jr.*
*Ralph Nader*
*Florence Nightingale*
*Albert Schweitzer*
*Mother Teresa*
*Sojourner Truth*
*Desmond Tutu*

North American edition first published in 1991 by
**Gareth Stevens Children's Books**
1555 North RiverCenter Drive, Suite 201
Milwaukee, Wisconsin 53212, USA

This edition is abridged from *Louis Braille: The inventor of a way to read and write that has helped millions of blind people communicate with the world*, copyright © 1989 by Exley Publications Ltd. and written by Beverley Birch. Additional end matter copyright © 1991 by Gareth Stevens, Inc. All rights reserved. No part of this book may be reproduced in any form or by any means without permission in writing from Gareth Stevens, Inc.

**Library of Congress Cataloging-in-Publication Data**

Lantier, Patricia, 1952-
  Louis Braille / Patricia Lantier's adaptation of the book by Beverley Birch. — North American ed.
    p. cm. — (People who made a difference)
  Includes index.
  Summary: The life of the nineteenth-century Frenchman, accidentally blinded as a child, who originated the raised dot system of reading and writing used by the blind throughout the world.
  ISBN 0-8368-0454-6
  1. Braille, Louis, 1809-1852—Juvenile literature. 2. Teachers, Blind—France—Biography—Juvenile literature. 3. Blind—Printing and writing systems—Juvenile literature. [1. Braille, Louis, 1809-1852. 2. Blind. 3. Teachers. 4. Physically handicapped.] I. Birch, Beverley. Louis Braille. II. Title. III. Series.
HV1624.B65L36    1990         686.2'82'092—dc20
[B]   [92]                                         90-9969

For a free color catalog describing Gareth Stevens' list of high-quality children's books, call

**1-800-341-3569 (USA) or 1-800-461-9120 (Canada)**

PICTURE CREDITS
Bridgeman Art Library — 8-9, 50-51/Musée Picardy, Amiens — 9/National Gallery of Capidomonte, Naples — 18/Victoria and Albert Museum — 4, 27; Chevojon Frères — 44; Exley Photographic Library — 21/Nick Birch — 10, 12 (both), 16 (below), 29, 30, 35 (both), 37 (both), 42, 43 (both), 47, 55 (both), 57; Fine Art Photographic Library — 16 (above), 22, 46; Giraudon — 22, 52; Alan Hutchinson Library/Maurice Harvey — 58 (left)/Juliet Highet — 58 (right); Tom Redman — cover illustration; Rex Features Ltd. — 38, 59 (above); Roger-Viollet — 28, 56 (below); Ann Ronan Picture Library — 14, 15, 24, 25, 48, 56 (above); Royal National Institute for the Blind — 6, 7, 33, 36, 41; Science Photo Library: Eunice Harris — 59 (below).

The publishers owe special thanks to Patricia Beattie and Alberta Lonergan of the American Foundation for the Blind, New York, and Bonnie Peterson of the National Federation of the Blind, Milwaukee.

**Series conceived and edited by Helen Exley**
Series editor, U.S.: Amy Bauman
Editorial assistants, U.S.: Scott Enk, Diane Laska, John D. Rateliff
Cover design: Kate Kriege

Printed in the United States of America

1 2 3 4 5 6 7 8 9 95 94 93 92 91

## PEOPLE
## WHO MADE
## A DIFFERENCE

*Bringer of
hope to
the blind*

# LOUIS
# BRAILLE

**Patricia Lantier**
**Beverley Birch**

Gareth Stevens Children's Books
**MILWAUKEE**

## Louis' quest

The dark room was very quiet. The only sounds were the creaking of iron beds, the rustling of blankets, the breathing of sleeping boys, and a low, knocking noise.

One boy was still awake. He sat upright in bed balancing a small board with papers on it across his knees. The boy pressed down on a piece of paper with a pointed instrument and made short, punching sounds.

It did not matter if the damp, cold room was dark. The boy could not see the dark. He could not see anything around the room. He could not even see the board across his knees.

The boy was blind. He had been blind for a long time. And all the other boys in the room with him were also blind.

The boy was very tired, but he did not let himself fall asleep. He kept punching the paper with his pointed instrument. He listened closely to the measured sounds of his movements.

Fourteen-year-old Louis Braille spent many nights awake with his board and paper. He often worked until the new day began. Then it was time for lessons, and he had no more free time.

*Opposite: In a gloomy, crowded neighborhood in Paris, much like the one shown here, a thirteen-year-old boy began to develop a unique method of writing and reading for blind people. His system has since become the international alphabet for blind people. It is named after him — braille.*

| A | B | C | D |
|---|---|---|---|
| • | •<br>• | • • | • •<br>  • |
| **E** | **F** | **G** | **H** |
| •<br> • | • •<br>• | • •<br>• • | •<br>• • |
| **I** | **J** | **K** | **L** |
|  •<br>• |  • •<br>• | •<br><br>• | •<br>•<br>• |
| **M** | **N** | **O** | **P** |
| • •<br>• | • •<br> •<br>• | •<br> •<br>• | • •<br>•<br>• |
| **Q** | **R** | **S** | **T** |
| • •<br>• •<br>• | •<br>• •<br>• |  •<br>• •<br>• | •<br>• •<br>• |
| **U** | **V** | **W** | **X** |
| •<br><br>• • | •<br>•<br>• • |  • •<br>• •<br> • | • •<br><br>• • |
| **Y** | **Z** | | |
| • •<br> •<br>• • | •<br> •<br>• • | | |
| and | for | of | the |
| • •<br>•<br>• • | • •<br>• •<br>• • | •<br>• •<br>• • |  •<br>•<br>• • |

*The genius of Braille's system is found in its simplicity. With the touch of a single fingertip, a blind person can recognize each letter of the alphabet.*

# A determined child

Louis had been working on this project for months. He had even taken it home during school vacation. There he worked outside in the warmth of the sun all summer. Passing villagers would say to each other: "Ah, there's young Louis at his pinpricks again!"

Louis *was* making little pinholes in his paper. They were very special pinpricks. These pinpricks would one day become the alphabet for blind people all over the world. With this system, blind people would be able to communicate better. They would not have to feel trapped in their darkness. But in Braille's time, people did not believe that blind people could do anything important.

Louis Braille did not know how successful his system of dots would become. After all, he was just a fourteen-year-old blind student in a special school in Paris. He knew, however, that there must be a way for blind people to read and write easily. There had to be a way for them to share all there was to learn in the world.

Louis Braille believed that blind people did not have to be cut off from a normal life. Louis knew this because he had not always been blind. Until he was three years old, he had his sight. But a terrible accident at that time took his sight forever.

Braille's six-dot system. To make the first ten letters of the alphabet (a-j), Braille used the top two rows of dots. For the next ten letters (k-t), he added one dot from the third row. For the last six letters (u-z), he used both dots from the third row, except for w, which is a reversed r.

## The saddler's son from Coupvray

Louis was born in Coupvray, France on January 4, 1809, to Monique and Simon-René Braille. When Louis was born, his mother, Monique, was forty-one years old; his father, Simon-René, was forty-four. Louis was the youngest of four children, who included Louis-Simon, Catherine-Joséphine, and Marie-Céline.

Coupvray was a village about twenty-five miles (40 km) east of Paris. The

*"Access to communication in the widest sense is access to knowledge.... We do not need pity, nor do we need to be reminded that we are [different]. We must be treated as equals — and communication is the way we can bring this about."*

*Louis Braille, 1841*

people of the village were mainly
farmers and tradespeople, and included
a tailor, a ropemaker, a weaver, a
locksmith, a doctor, a pharmacist, and a
midwife.

Louis' father, Simon-René, was a
saddler. He made saddles and harnesses.
Simon-René's father had also been a
saddler. Simon-René hoped his two sons
would go into this work, too.

This French country village is typical of the villages of Braille's childhood. In such villages, the change of seasons controlled life — the planting of and caring for the crops, the success or failure of the harvests. In celebration of harvest time, the residents of Coupvray sang the same songs and danced the same dances as generations before them had done.

Louis' family led a simple, ordinary life. They owned their farmhouse and seven and a half acres (3 ha) of land. Simon-René's workshop was also on this land. The Brailles were not rich, but there was always plenty of food to eat. They had many friends.

The family lived on a road called Chemin des Buttes. It was later renamed Rue Louis Braille. The stone farmhouse

had a huge roof, heavy oak doors, and a large chimney. Louis spent his early days playing in the farmhouse and talking with his mother while she worked.

He often visited his father in the workshop. To a curious little boy, the shop seemed a wonderful place. It smelled of leather, and bridles, reins, and straps hung everywhere. In the middle of the room stood a large workbench. It was lined with many shiny tools, such as knives and awls. Many of them were very sharp. This was where Louis' father did most of his cutting work.

*Opposite: Louis Braille may have been blinded by an awl or a knife. This painting by A. Harfort shows Louis reaching for a saddler's knife. The painting now hangs in what was once Louis' father's workshop. The Braille family home in Coupvray, France, is preserved as a museum.*

## The plunge into darkness

No one knows for sure just how Louis' accident happened. Nor is the exact date known. But it happened sometime in the year 1812. Many people told the story as they remembered it.

It is thought that the playful three-year-old boy climbed onto his father's big workbench when his father was not looking. Simon-René had probably stepped outside, perhaps to talk with someone about work. Louis probably reached for a knife or awl. Maybe he wanted to cut leather like his father. Soon after, people nearby heard screams coming from the workshop. Louis was crying, and blood poured down his face. His hands had slipped, and the sharp tool had cut into his eye.

*Above: The saddler's
tools belonging to
Simon-René Braille
are still on display in
his workshop.*

*Right: These steps lead
to the cellar of the
Braille farmhouse.*

# Permanent blindness

Louis' frightened parents did all they could for the boy. They washed his bleeding eye and bandaged it. When they were able to stop the bleeding, they took Louis to the doctor.

Unfortunately, doctors in those days did not know much about preventing infection. No one knew what to do for the little boy. Helplessly the doctor and the Braille family watched as Louis' eye became red and puffy. Soon, the whole eyelid was swollen. An infection developed and spread to the other eye.

Everything became blurry for Louis. He began to drop things, bump into furniture, and stumble constantly. His family took him to an eye doctor in a nearby town, but the doctor could not help. Louis' sight got worse each day. Eventually, he lost all sight in both eyes.

# Louis adapts

Louis' whole body began to adjust to the loss of sight. So he began to use his other senses more. Hearing became especially important. He listened carefully to noises outside and learned to recognize voices and footsteps.

Louis also developed a keen sense of touch. He could often tell what objects were just by touching them. He was able to sort shapes and widths of leather for his father. He could sort vegetables and eggs for his mother and sisters as they prepared for the weekly market.

Louis began to adapt to his dark world. There, sounds, smells, and his fingertips were his guides. No longer did he bump about the house. He knew people by their voices. He even knew which dog was barking and whose cart had rolled up to the workshop.

## The enemy comes to Coupvray

There was bad news in Coupvray in 1814. For years, France, led by Emperor Napoleon Bonaparte, had been at war

*For centuries, most blind people rarely ventured from their homes and families to experience the world or earn a living. A few blind people would occasionally make a few coins playing music, as shown in this picture.*

with various other European nations. These wars were called the Napoleonic Wars. Through them, Napoleon extended his empire across Europe in the early 1800s. But by 1813, his control was weakening. At that time, the armies of Austria, Russia, and Prussia combined to beat the French army.

By early 1814, the French army was in full retreat, trying to make it back to the capital city of Paris. On January 2, 1814, the French army arrived in Coupvray and demanded supplies from the villagers. By late February, the army had taken 1,200 bundles of hay, 706 loaves of bread, 405 bushels of oats, and most of the village horses and cows.

By April, the allied forces captured Paris, and then forced Napoleon to leave the country. Louis XVIII became the king of France. That month, the Russian army also came to Coupvray. The Russian soldiers also wanted food, horses, cows, wagons, and other supplies for their men. Simon-René was kept busy repairing saddles and harnesses for the foreign soldiers.

For two years, enemy soldiers became part of life in Coupvray. Sixty-four different soldiers stayed at the Braille house in that time. Louis' life echoed with new voices, strange footsteps, and the whispering of the French people. Everywhere they whispered about what

*There were few careers for blind people during Braille's lifetime. At best, they could learn some simple craft like the basketry being done by this blind boy.*

was happening to their country. The last of the soldiers finally left in 1816. Then the villagers worked hard to return to a normal life.

## A friend

In Louis' sixth year, a new priest came to the parish in Coupvray. Abbé Jacques Palluy visited each family in the village. He soon knew the Brailles very well.

Palluy especially liked Louis. The priest and the little boy became close friends. Louis often visited Palluy in his garden where the priest taught Louis many things. He taught the boy to recognize the smells and textures of different flowers. He described the sounds of birds and animals. He talked about the seasons of the year and the differences between night and day.

Louis loved these lessons. Soon he could recognize birds by their songs. He could feel the coolness of night before anyone else could.

## Louis starts school

In time, Louis was old enough to start school. In those days in France, most blind children did not go to school. Most people believed there was no reason to give lessons to them. It was even more unusual for blind children to attend the same school as sighted children.

But Palluy wanted to help Louis find a way to live on his own. He knew that Louis was very smart and was sure that the boy could learn just by listening to the teacher in class. So he went to see the village schoolmaster.

The schoolmaster, Antoine Bécheret, was also a newcomer to Coupvray. He was an eager young teacher who did not care what people thought. He agreed with Palluy. He thought that teaching the blind boy was a good idea.

So Louis went to school each day with one of his friends. He sat on a bench in front of class and listened eagerly to the

*Opposite, above:
Defeated at the Battle of Leipzig in October 1813, French Emperor Napoleon Bonaparte retreated toward Paris. Along the way, the troops seized supplies from villages like Coupvray. In the early months of 1814, news of the battles to the east and south of Coupvray upset the villagers. Then came the news that Napoleon was no longer in power. This picture shows the French in retreat after their final defeat by British and Prussian forces at Waterloo in June 1815.*

*Opposite, below:
The countryside surrounding Coupvray.*

*For centuries, most blind people were given little if any education. Most sighted people viewed blindness as a form of stupidity, a punishment, or something to be mocked. This painting by Pieter Brueghel portrays the blind leading the blind.*

teacher. He seemed to understand and remember everything he heard. A whole new world opened for Louis. He refused to believe that he could not live a full life because he was blind.

## What future for Louis?

Louis had dreams for his future. However, he really did not have many choices. There was little hope for blind people in those days. They could not easily study the same way sighted people could. Often, they were not taught skills with which to make a living.

Louis' parents worried about the time when they would no longer be able to

care for him. At that time, blind people had to depend on others for everything. Some were supported by their families or wealthy relatives. But many had to beg on the streets to survive.

## A special school in Paris

One day, the young schoolmaster Bécheret remembered that Paris had a special school for the blind. Palluy decided to try to enroll Louis in the special school.

Palluy also went to see the Marquis d'Orvilliers, a nobleman who often helped the poor people of Coupvray. The priest asked him to help send Louis to the

*This painting shows a school like the one in Coupvray that Louis Braille attended.*

*"Homeless blind people of all ages roamed the streets of most large towns, and even well-educated men and women seemed to find it amusing to watch them groping their way and bumping into buildings. They would throw things at them or trip them up, and then burst into laughter."*

Norman Wymer,
The Inventors

school in Paris. The marquis agreed to help. He also knew about the school for blind children. He had even met the founder, a man named Valentin Haüy.

Years before in 1786, Haüy had attended the Christmas celebration at the Royal Court of Versailles. Haüy had surprised the king and his guests with a group of blind children who could read and do arithmetic. The marquis had also attended this celebration and had been impressed with the children. He even donated money to Haüy's school.

Palluy begged the marquis to write to the director of the school. The marquis wrote at once, asking if Louis could become a pupil there. The director of the Royal Institution for Blind Children, Dr. Sebastien Guillié, soon wrote back to the marquis. The school had decided to accept Louis.

## The journey to Paris

So on February 15, 1819, ten-year-old Louis went to Paris to attend the Royal Institution for Blind Children. That special day was misty and cold in Coupvray. Louis and his father took a stagecoach out of the nearby town of Meaux. This coach would travel twenty-five miles (40 km) to Paris.

Louis was very excited. He was also scared and confused. He had waited a long time for an opportunity like this.

Would he like the school? It was so far away. Would he make new friends? Would he be able to find his way around?

Louis and his father talked a great deal on the journey. Louis' father described the countryside so that Louis could share in the beauty. Simon-René was very worried, however. He hoped that he and Louis' mother had made the right decision about the school.

Louis was still very young to be so far from home. Paris was a huge, noisy city full of strangers. It was so different from Coupvray. Simon-René knew, however, that Louis needed to learn a skill. The school taught many trades including those such as knitting, spinning, shoemaking, basketry, and ropemaking.

Louis and his father rode the stagecoach for four hours. It stopped at the edge of the city. Now they would have to find their own way to the school.

They walked to the Latin Quarter. This area of Paris was famous for its many schools. Louis' school was located on the Left Bank of the Seine River. Louis and his father walked until they found the school at 68 Rue Saint-Victor.

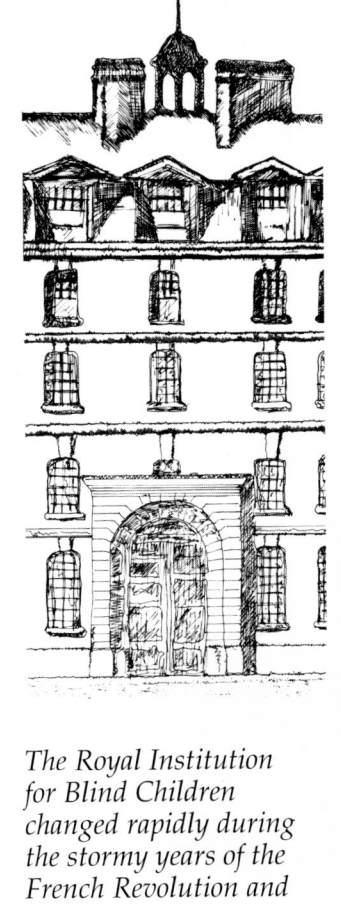

*The Royal Institution for Blind Children changed rapidly during the stormy years of the French Revolution and the years following. Valentin Haüy's reputation also rose and fell with the political changes sweeping the country.*

## 68 Rue Saint-Victor

The school building at 68 Rue Saint-Victor was dark and damp. The stairs were old, and the halls were narrow. The air was not as clean as in Coupvray.

Dr. Guillié, director of the school, met Louis and his father. He told them not to worry. There were many people who would take care of the boy. Simon-René hugged his son and left for Coupvray. Now Louis was really alone. Strangers he could not see were all around him.

*In 1819, Louis' journey to Paris took four hours by stagecoach. Although he had often listened in Coupvray as the stage-coach driver talked about Paris and the countryside, this was Louis' first ride in a stagecoach.*

## Strange surroundings

Dr. Guillié took Louis into the classroom right away. Louis heard the other pupils stand up when he walked in. He was

very frightened. For a moment he stood very stiff and still.

The teacher led Louis to a seat, and the class continued its lesson. Louis became absorbed in what his teacher was saying. Soon he stopped feeling scared and shy. By the end of class, he could answer all the teacher's questions about the lesson.

After class, Louis was afraid again. The teacher introduced him to the other students. Louis tried to remember their names and voices, but everything was loud and confusing.

Later Louis went to the boys' dormitory and unpacked his bag. As he put his belongings under his bed, he could feel the other boys all around him. This was his new home.

*"When [Louis Braille] first came to the house, a certain childish gravity was remarkable in him, and this was well suited to the delicacy of his features and the gentleness and intelligence of his expression."*
Dr. André Pignier,
Biographical Notes on
Three Former Professors
of the Institution for
Blind Children

## A new life

Louis soon made a friend. His name was Gabriel Gauthier, and he was a year older than Louis. Gabriel showed Louis around the halls and stairways. He explained how everyone lived. Little by little, Louis learned about the school.

The Braille family sent letters to Louis every week. Someone at the school read the letters to him. Soon he began to feel more comfortable. The school became his own special place.

Louis adjusted to his new life very quickly. He could soon find his own way around the building. He knew how

*"There were sixty pupils, and the head-master treated them with great severity, punishing the boys for the [smallest offenses]."*
Norman Wymer,
The Inventors

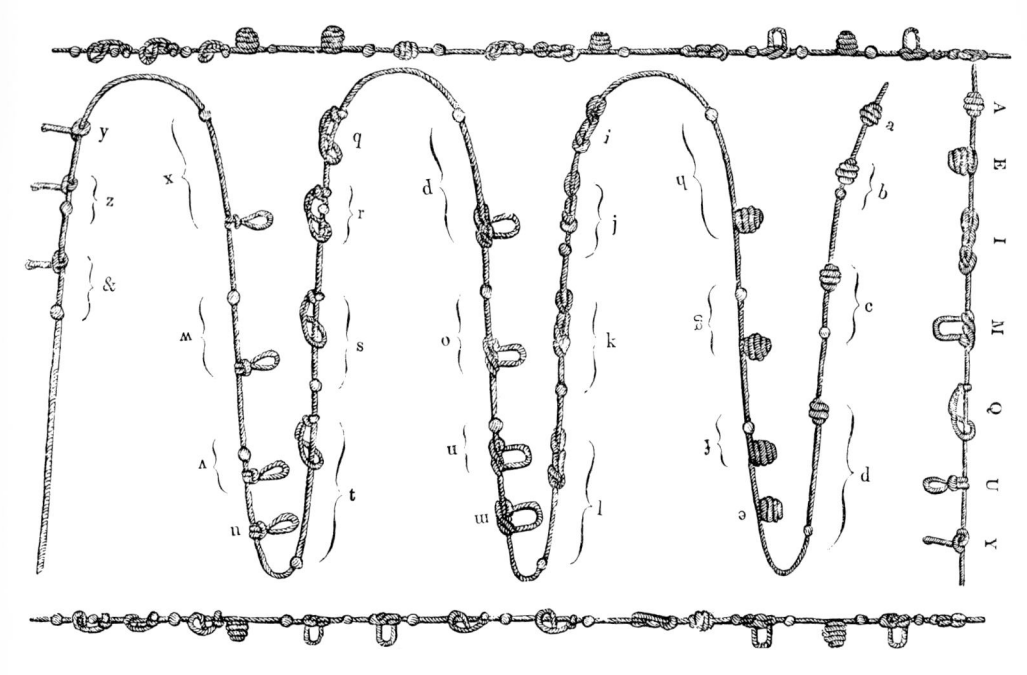

*Over the centuries, people in different countries had tried to find ways of communicating the alphabet to blind people. Using the unique method pictured above, blind people could read letters by feeling the pattern of the knots in a string.*

many steps it took to get from one place to another. He learned to recognize the voices of the students and teachers around him.

In school, Louis learned geography, history, arithmetic, and grammar. For most of the lessons, the teachers spoke to the students, and the students repeated what they heard. But there were also books written and printed especially for blind students.

## Haüy's books for blind people

Valentin Haüy had developed a way to print books for blind people. First, he made large lead letters, or type. Then he pressed heavy paper over the letters. In this way, letters were raised, or embossed, above the surface of the page.

These letters could then be felt by the reader's fingers.

There were only a few of these books in the school. They were very difficult to make. It took weeks to make a few copies of just one page. The books were big and clumsy. Each page was made of two pieces of paper pasted together. There were raised letters on each side. Some of the books were about religion. Others were grammar books written in different languages.

Louis was very excited when he first felt the raised letters under his fingers. But his excitement soon turned to frustration. Reading was very slow. He had to trace each letter of every word with his fingertips. Then he had to remember the letter while he went to the next one. It was easy to forget the first letters by the time he reached the last.

*Valentin Haüy's books for blind people were as large as the book pictured above. A book printed with Haüy's system was bulky and often required several volumes.*

## A talented pupil

Louis took lessons in basketry, knitting, and slippermaking. He enjoyed them all. But his favorite classes were the music classes. The school brought in teachers from the Paris Conservatory of Music to give lessons. These talented instructors taught the students to play flute, bassoon, piano, and organ.

Louis found that he loved music. He also discovered that he was skilled at it. Very quickly, he learned to play both the piano and organ. Making beautiful sounds gave him a sense of peace.

## A new director

In 1821, the school got a new director. The students did not know why Dr. Guillié left, but they were not very sad to see him go. Guillié was a harsh man. He had made many rules for the children, and he was very strict.

The new director was André Pignier. He was quite different from Dr. Guillié. Pignier was a dedicated man who was interested in every student's progress.

There was another reason for the students to be excited. Valentin Haüy was coming to visit. The man who had founded the school had not visited it for many years.

The French government had not approved of many of his decisions concerning the school over the years. Because of this, Haüy had accepted an invitation to work with blind students in Russia. He stayed there eleven years, finally returning to Paris in 1817. Soon after, he tried to visit his old school, but Dr. Guillié did not welcome him.

In 1821, with Guillié gone, things were different. Now the new director, Pignier, and his staff wanted to honor the man who had worked so hard to help others.

But Pignier and his staff knew that Haüy did more than offer education to

*Over the years, some blind people have earned livings as musicians. In this painting, a blind bagpipe player sets to work. Braille loved music and was skilled at playing the organ and piano. This talent might have provided a future for him if he had not invented the braille system.*

blind children. He proved to the world that blind people were not stupid just because they could not see. He made people understand that blind people deserved the same opportunities as anyone else.

## The founder's gift to the blind

Haüy had not always known about the hard lives of blind people. One day he saw a group of blind musicians act as clowns. They wore dunce caps and donkeys' ears and huge cardboard

*"What the blind so passionately desire and expect from us is that we should draw them into the great family circle of mankind where they will be but one link in the same human chain, ordinary men and women."*
    *Jean Roblin,*
    *in* Louis Braille

glasses. They made noises on old musical instruments. The sheets of music were turned the wrong way. The crowd laughed and made jokes.

This experience shocked twenty-six-year-old Haüy. He decided to do something to change people's attitudes. He did not think it was right for anyone to laugh at blind people. Educating them would be one way to help.

François Lesueur was Haüy's first pupil. Lesueur had been blind since he was six weeks old. For years the blind boy had begged on the streets of Paris. Haüy offered Lesueur a home and his first lessons. He also promised to pay the boy as much money as he would get begging in the streets.

Lesueur began to study with Haüy in 1784. Haüy began by teaching the boy to read. He used wooden letters that he could move around to form words. It worked — Lesueur learned to read! The boy could also recognize the imprint of letters on the back side of a page. This gave Haüy the idea to emboss several pages. He brought Lesueur to the Royal Academy, a group of France's best scholars and scientists. They were amazed at the boy's ability to read.

## A school for blind children

In time, Haüy's dream came true. The world had its first school for blind

*At the fair at St. Ovid in 1771, Valentin Haüy saw blind people clowning to the laughter of the audience. In earlier times, blind people had been considered useless. Many were killed at birth or abandoned to die when they grew old.*

children. Twenty-four pupils moved into an old house in Paris. At Christmas, they presented their skills at Versailles. Many people donated money. The government stepped in to help the school in 1791.

However, governmental control became too strong. Napoleon ordered the school to join with another building, a hospital for blind people. In addition, Haüy was fired.

After many years, the school was independent again. Haüy, however, had never been allowed to visit the place he had worked so hard to build. Pignier would change this.

## Haüy visits the school

Haüy was an old man in his seventies when Pignier invited him to pay an official visit to the school. The children did their best to please him.

Louis remembered that visit for the rest of his life. He felt Haüy's happiness all around him. The children proved Haüy was right. They were not stupid just because they could not see. They played music, recited poetry, and sang a special song for him. They wanted to thank Haüy for opening up a wonderful world to them.

## Barbier's dots and dashes

Charles Barbier was a captain in King Louis XVIII's army. He came to Pignier

*This statue of Valentin Haüy with François Lesueur now stands on the grounds of the National Institution for Blind Children in Paris. It honors that first act of compassion by Valentin Haüy, when he took Lesueur as his pupil.*

*This text is printed in the large embossed letters developed by Valentin Haüy. These books were large and heavy. Some subjects needed as many as twenty volumes, each weighing about twenty pounds (9 kg).*

with a new idea. He had invented a system of writing using only raised dots and dashes. He had developed it so that military orders could be passed along secretly at night. He called the system "night writing."

Captain Barbier had seen blind students reading at a museum in Paris. They used Haüy's heavy, embossed books. The captain saw how slowly the children had to read since the letters were hard to trace.

Captain Barbier wanted blind people to use his new system. He explained the method to Pignier. It was renamed *sonography*. It did not use single letters to spell out words. Instead, groups of dots and dashes expressed whole sounds. Up to this time, many people had tried to develop reading systems for the blind. However, no method had really worked.

The use of dots was something new. Other systems were all based on the alphabet used by sighted people. These new dots could be felt instead of seen.

Soon after speaking with Barbier, Pignier called a meeting of the entire school. No one knew what the meeting was about, but they knew it must be important. They were all very surprised to hear about Captain Barbier's invention. Pignier explained the new method to them. He passed around a few embossed pages of dots and dashes for the pupils to touch.

*"Like so many of the inventions that have been blessings to mankind, it came about accidentally. Opening up the world of written language to the blind was the furthest thing from the mind of the man [Charles Barbier] who devised the basic concept that made it possible."*
Frances A. Koestler,
The Unseen Minority:
A Social History of
Blindness in the
United States

## Louis learns the system

All of the students were curious and could hardly wait to feel the new pages. They slowly realized that it was easy to tell the various shapes apart.

Everyone was excited. Some of the children were afraid to learn something new. Others knew it would be faster than the old method. Many also realized they could learn to write with this system.

Louis was very quick to learn sonography. He soon knew all the charts of dots and dashes. He also learned how to use the writing device that Barbier had developed for this system.

The equipment was very simple to use. A special ruler with seven grooves was the main piece. To write, a student put a sheet of paper over this ruler. A special clip fit over the paper and slid along the ruler. In the sliding clip, there were little windows. The writer used the windows to place dots on the paper.

The students used a stylus to make dots and dashes. A stylus is a slim, pointed instrument with a round handle. Students used a stylus to punch down on the paper. Because of the grooves in the ruler, the dots stood out like bumps on the back of the paper. The writer moved from right to left. The words could then be read from left to right when it was turned over.

## Problems with Barbier's system

The children liked Barbier's system. Louis and Gabriel spent many hours writing sentences to each other and reading them back. But Louis soon realized that there were problems with sonography. It was only designed to represent words as a collection of sounds. So students could not spell with it. There were no punctuation symbols, such as commas or periods. Students could not write numbers, do arithmetic, or write music.

And there were so many dots for a single word! Each symbol might be as many as six dots deep. A single syllable of a word might need as many as twenty dots. There were too many dots for the students to feel with one finger. It was also hard to remember all the symbols.

Barbier's system was obviously much better than the embossed letters of Haüy. The students, however, soon agreed that there were too many dots in each word. They felt that the dots still didn't allow for a full expression of ideas.

## Louis meets Captain Barbier

Louis tried his best to improve Barbier's system. He spent many hours on experiments that seemed to work. He showed his findings to Pignier. The director was impressed. He said Louis should talk to Captain Barbier.

The captain met with Louis. He agreed that some small improvements were useful. He did not agree that his system needed basic changes. Louis said that there should be fewer dots and that spelling and punctuation should be added to the system.

The captain did not think these blind children needed such a complicated system. What they needed was a basic way to communicate with the world. He felt that anything more was a waste of time and energy. Captain Barbier did not understand what Louis was trying to say. The boy wanted more than basic

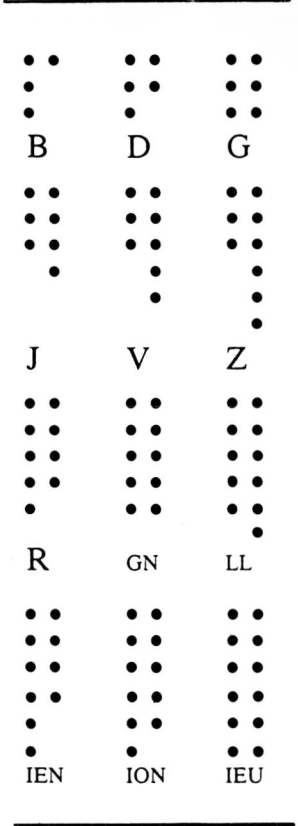

*Examples of Barbier's sonography are seen above. The dots refer to a grid of six lines across by six rows down, in which Barbier placed sounds. The dots marked the position of each sound in this grid. Students counted the number of dots in the first column to find out which row down. Then they counted those in the second column to find out which line across.*

communication. He wanted to be able to read and write complex thoughts and share them with others.

## Louis experiments

Captain Barbier said that his system was good enough. Louis gave up trying to convince him. Instead, he decided to experiment on his own. Louis Braille was now thirteen years old. He worked whenever he had a free moment during the day. He worked again at night. He even worked on the project the entire summer at home in Coupvray.

Louis wanted all the dots in each symbol to fit under one fingertip. He also had to arrange the dots and dashes in ways that were clearly understood. Every group of dots had to be different.

## The dawn of braille

Louis' alphabet was ready in October of 1824. A new school year had just begun. He had found a way to form letters, punctuation marks, and mathematical signs. His entire system used only six dots and some small dashes. The cluster of dots for each sign was small enough to be felt all at once with one finger.

Louis' friends were very excited. Groups of students gathered as he wrote faster than they ever thought possible. Pignier called Louis to his office. He wanted to watch the boy work. The

34

*Above: Braille's personal dominoes. The dots were removed to leave small dents that he could feel with his fingers.*

*Left: A Barbier ruler for writing adapted for Louis' six-dot system is shown on the left. On the right is an original Barbier ruler. The rulers are lying on an early version of Braille's alphabet, one that still included the dashes he later removed.*

director could hardly believe what Louis was doing. The system was simple and clear, and it used just six dots. Louis, however, had found sixty-three ways to use these six dots. Louis told the director that there were still some details to solve. Pignier congratulated the boy and told him to continue his experiments.

The other students learned Louis' system quickly. There were very few problems with it. Pignier had Captain Barbier's rulers changed to work with Louis' alphabet.

Pupils could now do many new things. They could take notes, write letters to each other, keep diaries, write stories, and copy anything they liked. It was the beginning of a wonderful new time for blind people.

*Below: St. Nicholas du Chardonnet was a nearby church that students from the institution attended. Holding on to a length of rope as a guide, they would make their way to Mass through the narrow streets of Paris.*

## Teacher and musician

Louis kept on experimenting with his "little system," as he called it. But he did not ignore his other activities at school. He continued to be a very good student.

In 1826, Louis began to teach algebra, grammar, and geography to the younger pupils. He was seventeen years old and still a student himself. He decided he liked teaching and that this would be his work in life. His students liked his gentle manner and concern for others.

Louis still enjoyed music. He became the organist at several churches in the

city. This gave him a chance to play the music he loved and to express his deep religious faith.

## The development of braille

Louis Braille's system developed and changed over the years. In 1827, he wrote a grammar book using his dot alphabet. Two years later, he wrote another one.

In 1828, he found a way to copy music. By now, he no longer used dashes in his alphabet. They were too difficult to write well with a stylus.

In 1829, Braille published the first book about his system. It was called *Method of Writing Words, Music, and Plain Songs by Means of Dots, for Use by the Blind and Arranged for Them*. This book marked

*"He never lost sight of this work. Never for an instant did he shirk the task of refining, developing and practicing his new way of writing and reading."*
Hippolyte Coltat,
Louis Braille's friend

*Below, left: The embossed music was produced by Valentin Haüy. It had all the drawbacks of the large embossed letters.*

*Below, right: Braille music of 1841. With this system, blind musicians could not only read music, but they could also write it.*

the formal birth of the braille system. Braille gave Captain Barbier full credit for the style of writing by dots. "We must say," he wrote, "that his method gave us the first idea of our own."

## An inspired teacher

Louis Braille officially became a teacher at the Royal Institution for Blind Children in 1828. By this time, he was nineteen years old. He taught grammar, geography, arithmetic, and music.

Braille tried to inspire his students. He remembered how it felt to be a young pupil at the school. He knew how to explain subjects so that his students understood their lessons. He also understood their special problems.

Life was much the same for Braille the teacher as it had been for Louis the student. He still wore the same school uniform, except that it was trimmed in gold braid. He still had to follow many rules. He could not leave the school without permission, and all his mail was read before going to him.

He did have his own room now. It felt strange not to hear the others sleeping all around him. Braille loved the peace and quiet of being alone. He could read and work whenever he wanted to.

Braille used his own alphabet to prepare lessons. He began work on a book of arithmetic. He continued to

*Opposite: A teacher guides the hands of a blind child along a piano keyboard. Many blind people have earned their living as singers, pianists, organists, and violinists. Most traditional schools for blind children stress musical skills.*

"With [Louis Braille] friendship was a conscientious duty as well as a tender sentiment. He would have sacrificed everything to it — his time, his health and his possessions."
Hippolyte Coltat, Louis Braille's friend

experiment with writing music. Braille was happy. He liked teaching, and he liked his friends. His two close friends, Hippolyte Coltat and Gabriel Gauthier, also became teachers at the school. They often sat together in Braille's room to discuss everything from school events to French politics.

## A time of loss

Three years later, in 1831, Louis Braille's father died. Simon-René had worried about his blind son even at the end of his life. Simon-René had written a letter to Pignier on his deathbed. In it, he asked the director never to abandon Louis.

Braille's father had reason to worry about his son. Louis Braille was often sick in the early years of the 1830s. By 1835, he knew he had a serious illness. He was always tired, even though he was just twenty five years old. He had fevers and a tightness in his chest. One night, Braille awoke with high fever. Blood filled his mouth. He called for help.

The school doctor discovered that Braille was bleeding internally. He determined that this was an early sign of a lung disease called tuberculosis.

At this time, doctors did not have a cure for this illness. In fact, they did not know much at all about tuberculosis. They only knew the symptoms — coughing, fever, and fatigue. They did not know yet that it was caused by a germ. Clean, fresh air might have helped Braille. The doctor, however, said only to rest more and eat well. And André Pignier tried to help by making Braille's classes smaller.

Braille now spent more time on research. In 1836, he added the letter *W* to his alphabet. An English student at the school asked him to do so. The French language did not have a letter *W*. He also published a revised edition of the book on his dot system in 1837. He still called it his "little system of writing by means of dots." He did not know that one day this "little system" would be known all over the world as braille.

## Raphigraphy

Braille also became interested in how blind people and sighted people could write to each other. His raised dots would not work because sighted people would have to learn the whole system.

In 1839, Braille developed a new way of using the forms of ordinary letters. He made these forms out of raised dots. Blind people could feel them, and sighted people could see them. Braille called this invention *raphigraphy*. Now the students could write to their parents and know the letters could be read.

A blind friend, François-Pierre Foucault, made a machine for printing

*Below are examples of Louis Braille's system of raphigraphy. This was a method of representing the letters of the ordinary alphabet with raised dots.*

*Above: This globe of the world uses braille. Braille can be applied to any device requiring the use of the alphabet, numbers, music, or scientific symbols.*

raphigraphy. He attached letters to levers that students would strike with their fingers. Letters would then leave imprints on paper. It was very much like an early typewriter!

## Opposition

Pignier tried to make braille the official system for the school. In 1837, the school's printing press had even produced a three-volume history of France. This was the first book ever to be

*Above left: A blind curator from the Valentin Haüy Museum in Paris operates a modern braille writer. By depressing the six keys in different combinations, a writer can emboss the paper with the necessary braille dots.*

*Above: François-Pierre Foucault, a blind inventor, developed this machine for printing Braille's raphigraphy. It is called a piston board.*

printed in braille. This was a big accomplishment for such a new system.

The governing body of the school would not agree to fully adopt the braille system. The Haüy system of embossed letters was still the official one. It would be expensive to change from Haüy to braille. All the books would have to be reprinted. Teaching methods would have to change.

Many people did not like braille because it used dots. They said blind people should use a sighted alphabet. Braille was disappointed by the lack of official support for his system.

Sixteen years after Braille developed the system, the board finally began to take notice. One member sent a note to Pignier saying, "This work strikes me as remarkable, and I think that Monsieur Braille ought to be encouraged." But Haüy's method was still the official one.

## Pignier is forced out

This was not the only disappointment Braille suffered that year. For some time, the vice principal of the school, P. Armand Dufau, had been trying to get rid of Pignier. Dufau wanted full control over the school. Because of the times, this was not difficult to do.

The French government had been through many changes. In 1824, Charles X became king when his his brother, Louis XVIII, died. Charles then tried to take power from the country's elected representatives. In 1830, the people revolted and forced Charles to leave. His cousin Louis Philippe then became king.

All these shifts in power made it a confusing time in France. It was especially difficult for people such as André Pignier. Like many people, his job was controlled by the government.

During this time, Dufau finally gained control of the school. In 1840, he told

*A bust captures Louis Braille. His friend Hippolyte Coltat described Braille as having curly blond hair. He was relaxed in manner yet purposeful in movement.*

school officials that Pignier's teaching methods were bad for the children. Officials forced Pignier to retire early and appointed Dufau as the new director.

Things were very different with Dufau as director. He wanted to show his authority. So he was strict and quick to punish the students. He also made many changes and didn't seem to care if the students were confused by them.

Dufau was not a strong supporter of the braille system. He believed that blind people should use the same alphabet as sighted people used. He said using a special alphabet separated blind people even more from a normal life.

*"Once [Louis Braille] had resolved to do something, he would carry it through conscientiously. It did not matter whether the task was pleasant or unpleasant, but only whether it was useful."*
Hippolyte Coltat,
Louis Braille's friend

## Braille's health gets worse

All the while, Braille's health was getting worse. In 1843, he stayed in bed for weeks at a time and sometimes coughed blood. Dr. Allibert, the school's doctor, said Braille needed more rest. Braille would have to stop teaching. Braille listened to the doctor's advice.

As the weeks went by, Braille's friends visited him every day. Warmer weather seemed to help a little. He started going on short walks with Gabriel Gauthier and Hippolyte Coltat. They sometimes visited Pignier, who lived near the school.

One day, Braille started bleeding again. Dr. Allibert said he should go home to rest. Braille stayed in Coupvray

*A painting by the famous French artist Jean Baptiste Camille Corot shows a typical country village during Braille's lifetime.*

for six months. He liked being with his family, and living in the country seemed to help his health. Everything was calm and quiet there.

Also in 1843, Antoine Bécheret died. Bécheret was the last of the three people who had helped Braille as a child. Abbé Palluy and the Marquis d'Orvilliers had died years before.

## Back to Paris

Braille returned to Paris in October 1843. He felt much better. But conditions at the school had grown much worse. As

*The Braille family house in Coupvray as it stands today. Both the house and Simon-René's workshop have been preserved as a museum.*

director, Dufau was changing the size of Valentin Haüy's embossed letters. He had even burned all of the old books printed in the original embossed alphabet. In fact, all twenty-six books printed by Guillié and the forty-seven books printed by Pignier had been burned. The students had to learn to read all over again.

Braille's dot alphabet was not a part of Dufau's new plan, except for writing music. But the students clung to the system and continued to use it among themselves outside of class for their own notes and letters. When Dufau discovered this, he forbid them to use it.

Joseph Gaudet was Dufau's new deputy at the school. He knew the students wanted to use the braille system. Gaudet believed that the students would benefit from braille and persuaded Dufau to consider the system.

## A new school

Many famous people visited the school for blind children. One was a poet and historian named Alphonse Marie Louis

*Blind guests arrive for a social gathering. Compare this situation to the one depicted in the painting by Brueghel on page 18 that also shows "the blind leading the blind."*

de Lamartine. In 1838, de Lamartine made a speech to the Chamber of Deputies about the poor living conditions on Rue Saint-Victor. The Chamber of Deputies was a branch of France's government, and de Lamartine was a member. The chamber voted to buy land on the Boulevard des Invalides and build a new school.

The new buildings were ready in 1843. The students on Rue Saint-Victor packed their belongings and moved from the old, dirty school. The new building was clean and airy. Louis Braille might not have gotten tuberculosis if he had spent his life in such a healthy space.

## Approval for Braille's system

The new school officially opened on February 2, 1844. A huge crowd of relatives and officials gathered for the ceremony. The school choir sang a song in tribute to Haüy. Pupils recited poetry and played music.

To everyone's surprise, Dufau then described Braille's system of writing with raised dots. The director explained the advantages of Braille's system over that of Barbier or Haüy. He gave full credit to Braille. The school had finally approved the dot system.

The work of the blind students with the braille system had paid off. Louis Braille's wonderful invention was

*"Yesterday I visited the Royal Institution for Blind Children. No description could give you a true idea of this building, which is small, dirty and gloomy; of those passages partitioned off to form boxes dignified by the name of workshops or classrooms, of those many tortuous, worm-eaten staircases, which, far from seeming suited to unfortunates who can guide themselves only by their sense of touch, are ... more like a challenge flung down to these children's blindness."*
Alphonse de Lamartine in his speech to France's Chamber of Deputies

*In 1843, the Royal Institution for Blind Children moved to a cleaner, airier part of Paris on the Boulevard des Invalides. The armed forces hospital, called Les Invalides, and the elegant gardens shown in this picture are at the northern end of this wide boulevard.*

officially accepted at last. Deputy Gaudet showed the audience just how braille worked. One of the blind girls wrote down some poetry read by a member of the audience. Another girl, who had not been in the room, came in and read the writing perfectly.

There was tremendous applause. Braille was very happy. The battle to have his system adopted was over.

## Dufau helps Braille

Director Dufau now seemed to have been

won over.  In the following years, he seemed to try to make up for his earlier harshness.  He even got permission to care for Braille at the school as the young man grew sicker.  By this time, Braille's cough was worse, and he tired easily. Dufau finally told him to stop teaching.

Braille kept himself busy.  He spent much of his time copying books into his dot alphabet for the school's library. Sometimes Braille asked students at the school to copy books for him.  He paid these assistants himself, then gave the

In 1848, revolutions occurred in France and Europe. In Paris, workers, students, and soldiers of the French National Guard declared the country of France a republic. They then toppled King Louis Philippe from the throne that he had held for eighteen years.

books to poor students who had no way to obtain reading materials.

Braille often helped his friends, too. In his room, he kept a small box containing his savings. When someone needed a loan for books or school tuition, he gladly lent the money. He knew these friends would pay him back one day. He even gave scholarships to blind students who were too poor to pay tuition.

Braille rested for three years. In 1847, the doctor said he could teach again. Braille loved to teach, even if he was tired most of the time. He spent the next three years happily teaching his classes and visiting his family in Coupvray.

# Braille's last years

By 1850, Braille was feeling very ill again. The director offered to let him stay at the school and teach a few piano lessons.

By December 1851, Braille knew he was dying. There was more internal bleeding. He could no longer get out of bed. Braille put his affairs in order. He left many of his belongings to his friend Coltat, who gave them to the students who loved Braille. Braille left the rest of his belongings to his mother.

Louis Braille died on January 6, 1852. It was two days after his forty-third birthday. Braille was buried at Coupvray. His final journey home was along the same road that he had first traveled to Paris with his father thirty-three years earlier.

Louis Braille became famous in the years following his death. People all over the world admired his courage and dedication. But even more than this, Braille's dot system helped millions of blind people to have better lives. With his system, they could read, write, and communicate. They could be productive members of society.

# Braille in the world

In 1854, France adopted braille as its official system for blind people. Other countries began to take notice. Teachers in Switzerland began to teach braille in

*"Despite his blindness, despite continual ill-health, despite the ill-will of others which delayed the recognition of his work ... he remained kindly, cheerful and faithful to his friends and to his ideal."*
Jean Roblin,
in Louis Braille

*"He remembered the little boy who used to guide him, the orderly who nursed him, the night-nurse who sat up with him and even the servant who cleaned his room. On the brink of death, as in his life, he was grateful to those who had helped him."*
Jean Roblin,
in Louis Braille

the 1850s. And the Swiss school for blind children at Lausanne printed the first book in braille outside France.

In some countries, such as Germany and England, teachers of blind students did not want to use braille. They tried many other methods instead. Most of these other systems were based on the embossed letters of the regular alphabet. This meant that blind people could only work with the system they were taught. They could not understand material from another reading system.

Finally, Dr. Thomas Armitage decided to do something. Armitage had founded the British and Foreign Association for Promoting the Education of the Blind. He knew that blind people were the only ones qualified to decide upon a single system. He organized a committee of blind people. The people on the committee would judge many methods and choose the best one. They chose braille. Most British schools for the blind had adopted braille by 1883.

*"The fact emerges that braille was not established through the influence of interested parties, but by an urge from within, by the enthusiasm of those who, using it themselves, had daily experience of its worth. . . . "*
*Pierre Henri,*
The Life and Work
of Louis Braille

## International fame

An important international meeting of European nations took place in Paris in 1878. Austria-Hungary, Belgium, Denmark, Britain, France, Germany, Italy, Sweden, and Switzerland had sent representatives. These people had looked at all the methods of printing and

writing for the blind. They wanted to establish only one system to be used all over the world. The members voted for the braille system.

The United States, however, continued to use more than one system. This caused confusion for students and teachers. The United States finally adopted the braille system after almost forty years of experimenting.

In 1929, eighteen nations adopted a braille system for music. This would have made Louis Braille very happy. He had spent many long years working on an accurate dot system for the beautiful music he loved so much.

In 1932, members from nearly one hundred countries accepted a British

*Above, left: This pocket watch was owned by Louis Braille. The glass can be lifted to feel the hands.*

*Above: This braille watch uses the braille system's six-dot code.*

braille system. Soon it was possible for any English-speaking blind person to write to any other English-speaking blind person. All material printed in British braille would be the same.

Today, the countries of the Far East, such as China and Japan, have their own braille systems. India, the Middle East, and Africa do, as well.

## Modern technology

In 1837, the National Institution for Blind Children printed a three-volume history of France. These were the first books ever to be printed in braille. At this time, small blocks of metal were inked for printing. Each block contained all six of Braille's dots. To form different letters, students at the Paris school had to break off any dots they did not need for that letter. Letters were then put into words.

By 1849, there were experiments in printing with a process called *stereotyping*. This process made it easier to print an entire page of embossed symbols at one time.

Finally, in the United States, Frank Hall invented the braille writer. This machine had six keys, one for each dot. Anyone could operate the machine by pressing several keys at the same time to make all the dots in a letter. People could now write up to ten letters a minute. This was twice as fast as before.

# Braille in the computer age

Over the years, people have continued to do research with braille. There have been a few changes in the original alphabet. Until the late 1950s, a sighted person trained in braille was always needed to copy books into the dot alphabet. But researchers in the United States developed a way to print braille in a computer. Now someone who does not know braille can still produce the correct type. Modern word processors also help to make this job easier.

Researchers have also developed machines that can electronically read a text printed in ink. These machines then change the text into braille with a computer's help. This process is four times faster than typing from a keyboard.

Research is still being done for the future of blind people. Special printers might one day send material on electronic tape directly to a library. The library might have a machine to change the tape into braille. Blind readers will then be able to read anything they want.

Personal computers have also opened up many possibilities. There are machines and programs that help a blind person to write and proofread. These programs use a braille keyboard and braille display. Blind people can get printed copy not just in braille, but also in ordinary type for sighted people.

*An example of the Moon system, developed by Dr. William Moon. This is one of the many written systems that competed with braille in the 1860s. The Moon system is the only one that still survives.*

*Opposite, above: Braille was accepted by an international conference of nations in 1878. After that, several inventors in different countries worked on developing machines for writing braille. Here a blind man writes with Mauler's braille machine of 1887.*

*Opposite, below: Students examine a braille globe.*

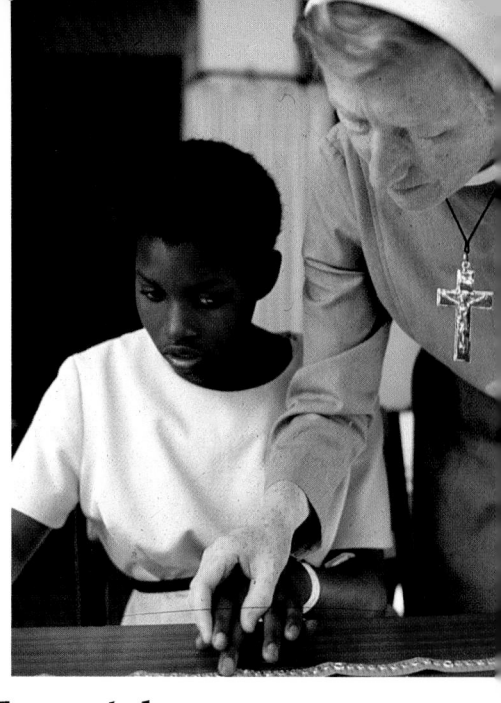

*Above: A South African man reads a braille version of the Bible.*

*Right: A blind Nigerian girl is shown a braille tape measure. Braille can be adapted for almost any language that uses the Roman alphabet and many that do not. At present, it has been adapted for more than fifty languages and dialects.*

## One of France's heroes

Louis Braille was honored by the world one hundred years after his death. In 1952, people from forty nations came to pay their respects to him at his grave in Coupvray. Then they traveled with his body on its last journey to Paris. Louis Braille was buried among other great people of France at the Panthéon.

One thing is certain. It does not matter where Louis Braille is buried. As long as blind people use braille to share in the joy and beauty of their surroundings, and to develop into educated, independent citizens of the world— his name will be remembered and honored.

*Upper left:
Students learn
to use braille
typewriters at
a school for
blind people.
Some braille
typewriters type
letters in braille.
Others type in
normal script.
Blind people can
usually write at a
rate of about ten
words per minute
by hand, but they
can double this
speed with a
mechanical
braille writer
with six keys.*

*Lower left:
Braille playing
cards have
the numbers
written in the
six-dot code.*

59

# To find out more . . .

## Organizations

The organizations listed below can answer questions about Louis Braille, the Braille system, blindness, and what is being done today to help visually-impaired people lead normal lives. Many of these organizations have state and local branches in addition to the national offices listed here, so check your local phone book. When you write these organizations, be sure to tell them exactly what you want to know. Also include your name, address, and age.

American Brotherhood for
  the Blind
1800 Johnson Street
Baltimore, Maryland  21230

American Council of the Blind
1010 Vermont Avenue NW
Suite 1100
Washington, DC  20005

Braille Institute of America
741 North Vermont Avenue
Los Angeles, California  90029

Canadian National Institute
  for the Blind
1931 Bayview Avenue
Toronto, Ontario  M4G 4C8
Canada

National Association to Promote
  the Use of Braille
3618 Dayton Avenue
Louisville, Kentucky  40207

## Books

The books listed below will help you learn more about Louis Braille and his system and what it's like being blind or visually impaired. Check your local library or bookstore to see if they have them or can order them for you.

### *About Louis Braille* —

*Louis Braille.* Stephen Keeler (Franklin Watts)
*Louis Braille: The Boy Who Invented Books for the Blind.* Margaret
  Davidson (Scholastic)

60

## About being blind or visually impaired —

*Child of the Silent Night: The Story of Laura Bridgeman.* Edith F. Hunter (Houghton Mifflin)
*Follow My Leader.* James B. Garfield (Scholastic)
*From Anna.* Jean Little (Harper & Row)
*The Gift.* Helen Coutant (Knopf)
*A Guide Dog Goes to School: The Story of a Dog Trained to Lead the Blind.* Elizabeth S. Smith (Morrow Junior Books)
*Guide Dog Winners.* Ed and Ruth Radlauer (Childrens Press)
*See You Tomorrow.* Miriam Cohen (Greenwillow)
*Seeing in the Dark.* Elizabeth R. Montgomery (Garrard)
*Seeing in Special Ways — Children Living with Blindness.* Thomas Bergman (Gareth Stevens)
*The Seeing Summer.* Jeanette Eyerly (Archway)
*Shelley's Day: The Day of a Legally Blind Child.* Candice C. Hall (Andrew Mountain)
*Through Grandpa's Eyes.* Patricia MacLachlan (Harper Junior)
*The Witch's Daughter.* Nina Bawden (G.K. Hall)

## List of new words

**antibiotic**
A chemical that can kill the germs that cause disease.

**awl**
A pointed tool used by a saddler or harnessmaker for making holes in leather. Awls are also used in woodworking.

**Bonaparte, Napoleon (1769-1821)**
A brilliant French general who became the leader of France in 1799. Under his leadership, the French army conquered most of Europe between 1800 and 1813.

**bushel**
A unit with which liquids and solids can be measured. One bushel equals about nine U.S. gallons (35 liters).

61

**Chamber of Deputies**
A special branch of the French government during the nineteenth century.

**congress**
As used in this book, a congress is a meeting of people interested in a certain topic, for example, blindness.

**Coupvray**
A small village 25 miles (40 km) east of Paris, in France. Louis Braille was born in Coupvray in 1809.

**grammar**
The study of the rules that help people write or speak a certain language properly.

**harness**
The leather and metal pieces that hook a horse or other animal to a cart, a plow, or other vehicle.

**Haüy, Valentin**
The founder of the world's first school for blind children in Paris, France. Haüy helped open the world to blind people, and encouraged sighted people to respect those who could not see.

**marquis**
A nobleman whose rank is higher than an earl and lower than a duke. The Marquis d'Orvilliers in France helped young Louis Braille attend school in Paris.

**midwife**
A woman who helps other women during childbirth. A midwife can help deliver babies when a doctor is not available.

**Panthéon**
A special building used as a tomb for a country's famous dead people. The Panthéon in Paris was designed in 1764.

**penicillin**
A special medicine, or antibiotic, used to treat infections.

**Prussia**
A former kingdom and state of Germany that covered land that is now part of Germany and Poland. In the early 1800s, Prussia became the central state in the powerful German Confederation. From this position, the king of Prussia, King William I, organized the German empire and became its emperor in 1871.

**raphigraphy**
Braille's name for his method of writing that made it possible for blind people to write to sighted people. In 1841, François-Pierre Foucault invented a machine for typing raphigraphy.

**saddler**
A skilled worker or craftsman who makes all kinds of equipment for horses.

**scholarship**
Money given to help a student continue his or her education.

**sonography**
A method of writing invented by Captain Charles Barbier in France for use in the military. This system of raised dots and dashes was used to pass military orders secretly at night. Knowledge of this system helped Louis Braille develop his own dot alphabet.

**stylus**
A sharp, pointed tool used for writing. Louis Braille used a stylus to make dots on paper.

**tuberculosis**
A contagious disease that attacks mainly the lungs. It can be acquired by drinking milk from infected cows or by breathing

in the germs coughed out by other people. The bacteria that cause the disease are killed by sunlight. But they can live in damp, dark conditions for weeks, so poor housing helps to spread this disease. Poorly nourished persons are much more likely to acquire the disease than well-nourished people are.

## Versailles

The name of both a city and a palace in France. The palace has many rooms, each with elegant furniture and expensive art objects. Its gardens are famous for their design and sculptures. The Versailles palace is located near Paris, and is a national museum.

# Important dates

**1784**    The Royal Institution for Blind Children, founded by Valentin Haüy, opens in Paris.

**1789**    The French Revolution begins. Haüy is dismissed as director of the school.

**1800**    On Napoleon's orders, the blind children are put into an asylum for people with other disabilities.

**1809**    **January 4** — Louis Braille is born in Coupvray, France. He is the fourth child of Simon-René and Monique Braille.

**1812**    Three-year-old Louis blinds one eye in an accident. An infection sets in, and he gradually loses all sight.

**1814**    Russian troops occupy Coupvray as Napoleon's empire falls. Captain Charles Barbier starts work on his writing system, called sonography.

**1815**    Jacques Palluy becomes the parish priest of Coupvray and starts teaching Louis. The Royal Institution for Blind Children reopens in Paris.

| 1816 | Antoine Bécheret offers Louis a place as a student in the Coupvray school. |
|---|---|
| 1819 | Louis, age ten, leaves for Paris to attend the Royal Institution for Blind Children founded by Haüy. |
| 1821 | Barbier demonstrates sonography to the institution. Dr. André Pignier becomes the institution's new director. |
| 1824 | At fifteen, Louis completes his first dot alphabet based on Barbier's invention of sonography. |
| 1827 | A French grammar book is transcribed using Louis' system. |
| 1828 | Braille becomes an assistant teacher at the institution. |
| 1829 | Braille publishes a booklet explaining his six-dot system. |
| 1833 | Braille gains a position as an organist at a nearby church. |
| 1834 | The governors of the institution refuse to allow the students to use Braille's alphabet. Braille demonstrates his six-dot system at the Exhibition of Industry in Paris. |
| 1835 | Braille shows the first signs of tuberculosis. |
| 1837 | Blind teachers and students at the institution produce the first book in the braille system. |
| 1838 | **May 14** — In a speech to the Chamber of Deputies, Alphonse Marie Louis de Lamartine condemns the conditions at the institution for Blind Children. The Chamber of Deputies votes to build a new building. |
| 1839 | Braille starts work with sighted assistants on machines that will print his dot system. |

**1840** P. Armand Dufau and the school directors force Dr. André Pignier to retire. Dufau becomes the new director.

**1841** François-Pierre Foucault invents a machine for typing raphigraphy.

**1843** Braille's health worsens. He goes to Coupvray to recover. **November** — The new school for blind children at 56 Boulevard des Invalides is finished.

**1844** **February 22** — The new school is officially opened.

**1847** Foucault, along with Louis Braille, finishes developing a braille typewriter.

**1850** Braille's tuberculosis gets worse. He reduces his teaching schedule to only a few music lessons.

**1851** Braille is so ill that he enters the institution's hospital.

**1852** **January 6** — Louis Braille dies at age forty-three. His body is taken to Coupvray to be buried.

**1854** France adopts braille as its official system for blind people.

**1878** An international congress decides braille is the best system for blind people and agrees to promote braille around the world.

**1949** India asks UNESCO — the United Nations Educational, Scientific, and Cultural Organization — to regulate braille for use in all languages. Over one hundred languages and hundreds of dialects can now be written in braille.

**1952** Braille's body is moved from Coupvray and reburied in the Panthéon in Paris.

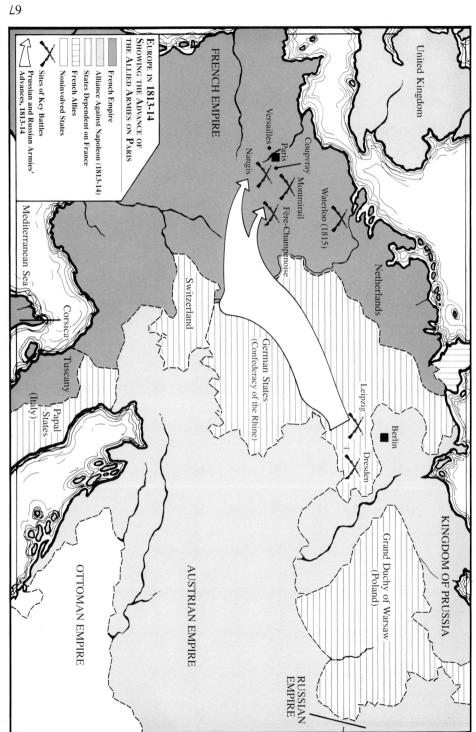

EUROPE IN 1813-14
SHOWING THE ADVANCE OF
THE ALLIED ARMIES ON PARIS

French Empire
States Dependent on France
French Allies
Noninvolved States

✗ Alliance Against Napoleon (1813-14)
✗ Sites of Key Battles
⬆ Prussian and Russian Armies'
Advances, 1813-14

FRENCH EMPIRE

Mediterranean Sea

Corsica

Tuscany

Papal
States

(Italy)

OTTOMAN EMPIRE

Switzerland

German States
(Confederacy of the Rhine)

AUSTRIAN EMPIRE

United Kingdom

Versailles
Paris
Nangis
Coupvray
Montmirail
Fère-Champenoise
Waterloo (1815)

Netherlands

Leipzig

Dresden

Berlin

KINGDOM OF PRUSSIA

Grand Duchy of Warsaw
(Poland)

RUSSIAN
EMPIRE

# Index